The Essential Handbook

of

VICTORIAN
ENTERTAINING

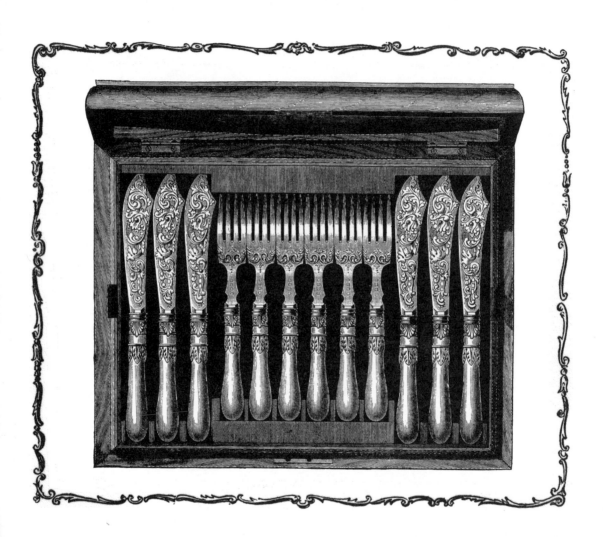

The Essential Handbook

of

VICTORIAN ENTERTAINING

Adapted by Autumn Stephens

A Bluewood Book

Bluewood Books
a division of The Siyeh Group, Inc.
P.O. Box 689
San Mateo, CA 94401

ISBN 0-912517-54-9

Printed in the USA

Adapted by Autumn Stephens
Designed by Giraffe-X, San Francisco, CA
Illustrations by Charles Dana Gibson and a host of
other notable artists of the Victorian Era.

TABLE OF CONTENTS

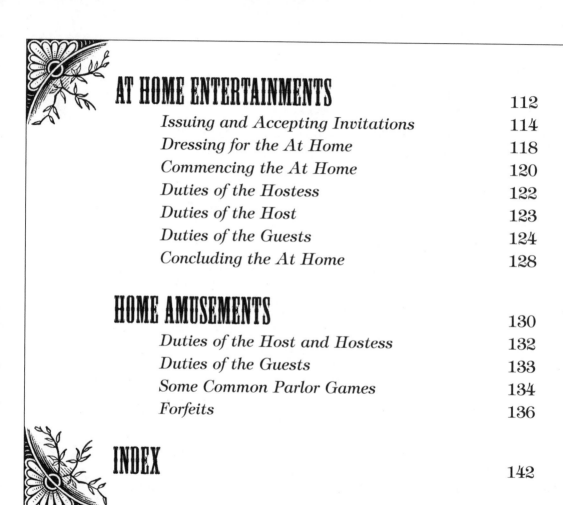

A Word to the Reader

or our genteel Victorian ancestors, there was no such thing as casual entertaining. Theirs, after all, was a world in which a minor misstep could ruin a gentleman's reputation—and even more definitively a lady's. For better or worse, ignorance was no excuse for bad behavior, as the all-important rules of social intercourse were copiously codified in myriad books of etiquette.

Ladies and gentlemen knew exactly what time of day to visit their friends, the time of which differed, by the way, from season to season. It went without saying that only the daintiest and tidiest of finger foods were offered at an afternoon tea party, so that guests could partake without soiling their gloves. (Oddly, gloves were a must while taking tea, but a big no-no at a fancy evening meal.) Married women were officially allowed to down five or six glasses of wine at a formal dinner, if they cared to do so, but the young and the single had to make do with three.

Drawn from the very best and most respected 19th century sources, this handbook will guide you through the ins and outs of Victorian entertaining. Now you, too, can learn how to host an authentic 19th century dinner party, what the perfect houseguest wears to breakfast on Sunday morning, and the circumstances under which a gentleman may attempt, with no blemish upon his good name, to kiss every woman in the room. And much, much more.

However, first, it must be said that even the most exuberant enthusiast of Victoriana, would scarcely endorse a reprisal of every cumbersome custom from the days of corsets and smelling salts. Yet, we should remember that the Victorian preoccupation with etiquette grew over time, becoming more sophisticated from the simple desire to adhere to a moral code of "do unto your neighbors as you would have them do unto you." To dismiss this obsession out of hand, or out of context, would surely be an error. Who, after all, can argue against being kind to our fellow human beings? Well, okay, we all know a few louts who can, but to those few we simply say: "You, sir, — are no gentleman! You, madam, are no lady!"

Party on!

SOCIAL VISITS

 ecent formalities are necessary even in the most unreserved friendships; they preserve the "familiar" from degenerating into the "vulgar." Disgust will very speedily arise between persons who bolt into one another's chambers, throw open the windows, and seat themselves without being desired to do so. Thus, on all occasions of social intercourse, common courtesy must be the absolute rule; it is not going too far to say that civilization depends upon it.

The Social Call

It is the custom in society for each lady, or group of ladies within a household, to devote one day a week to receiving calls. By the pleasant custom of calling and receiving calls, old friendships may easily be preserved, and new ones established. In paying calls during the day, lady callers go alone, or are accompanied by other ladies, as it is understood that gentlemen will be occupied with professional matters during that time.

The Calling Card

Your calling card should be of paper that is white, heavy, plain, and unruled, elegantly engraved with your name and address. Highly decorated or gaudy cards betray ill breeding. If a lady is unmarried, it is the fashion to affix "Miss" before her name on her calling cards. The cards of gentlemen are half the size of those used by ladies. For visits of condolence, the card should be of the type known as a mourning card, with a narrow mourning border.

Occasions Upon Which to Call

Proper etiquette does not allow one to tender regrets, express thanks, or otherwise dispatch one's social obligations with a written message. In nearly every case, a personal visit, or at least the attempt to make one, is necessary. (It does sometimes occur that the hostess is otherwise engaged when one comes to call.) Yet, such calls need not be an onerous duty; a stay of ten to twenty minutes is sufficient to convey one's meaning and engage in a bit of pleasant conversation. Indeed, to linger more than half an hour is considered downright rude.

When you have received an invitation to a party, it is imperative to call upon the person who issued it within the week, whether or not you accept.

It is obligatory to call upon your friends prior to departing from town for an interval, as well as upon returning.

Calls of condolence are made within a week after the event that occasioned them.

Calls of congratulations are made upon the engagement or marriage of a friend, the birth of a baby, the appointment of a friend to any office or dignity, or upon a friend's deliverance of a public oration.

You must pay a return call within three days of another party's first call upon you.

If a person with whom you are not acquainted, but who belongs to your own class of society, takes up residence in your town, or makes an extended visit to one of your friends, you are obliged to make the first call. Since this person is bound to frequent the same establishments that you do, and to circulate in your social set, you will naturally wish to begin your acquaintance on the proper footing.

THE HOURS OF THE SOCIAL CALL

What a grievous error it would be to interpret the term "morning call" in a literal sense, and go about knocking on doors before the sun is quite high in the sky. For of course morning calls do not mean, as the term would imply, calls made before noon. Ladies customarily occupy themselves with

private and domestic matters during the earliest hours of the day, and rest assured that few would welcome an intrusion during this precious interval.

Rather, a morning visit should be paid between the hours of 2:00 P.M. and 4:00 P.M., in winter, and 2:00 P.M. and 5:00 P.M. in summer. By observing this rule you avoid intruding before the luncheon is removed, and leave in sufficient time to allow the lady of the house an hour or two of leisure for her dinner toilette.

Evening calls must not be made later than 9:00 P.M., nor continued longer than 10:00 P.M. It is assumed that a husband and wife will pay evening calls together. As on any occasion when a gentleman accompanies a lady, it falls to the lady to determine the precise length of the visit. Evening calls should not be frequent, nor much protracted, and certainly never paid upon any person with whom one is not well acquainted.

Dressing for Social Calls

For the Hostess

When receiving morning calls in her own home, the hostess should wear her prettiest house gown to do honor to her visitors.

A lady should always be prepared for casual callers in the evening, even when not receiving. Wise matrons, it is said, advise their sons to select rainy evenings for calling upon their young lady friends, so that they may find out who are fit to be seen when not expecting company. The dress for evening calls should be tasteful and becoming, made with a certain amount of ornament, and worn with lace and jewelry. Artificial flowers are out of place, and glittering gems are only worn on more important occasions.

For receiving New Year's or other special calls, the dress should be rich, and may be elaborately trimmed.

For Lady Callers

When calling, in either the daytime or evening, a lady should wear her handsomest street gown, wrap, and hat, a costume such as she would wear to church or an afternoon reception. If she has a carriage at her command, she may dress more elegantly than if she were on foot.

For Gentlemen Callers

A gentleman retains his "walking" or "morning" suit until 6:00 P.M. Proper morning attire consists of gray, striped trousers, black vest, and black coat. A black frock coat with black pants is not considered a good combination. While a top hat must be worn for formal calls, a crowned bowler is not out of place on other occasions.

As to evening wear, a gentleman need not sit down and give more than a moment's thought to his wardrobe, or to whether the Smiths will notice if he should wear the same attire three times running. Fashion has ordained for him that he shall always be attired in a black dress suit in the evening, regardless of his destination.

COMMENCING THE SOCIAL CALL

For the Hostess

A well-bred person always receives visitors at whatever time they may call. If you are occupied and cannot afford to be interrupted, you should instruct the servant to say that you are "engaged." The form "not at home" sometimes employed by ladies cannot be too strongly condemned. However much one may try to justify it, the fact remains that it is a falsehood.

If the servant once admits a visitor within the hall, you must receive him at any inconvenience to yourself.

A lady should never keep a visitor waiting more than a minute or two, at the most.

Upon important occasions, it is well for a lady to be assisted by a gentleman in the reception of guests.

For the Callers

When paying a call, present your card to the servant who opens the door. The servant will convey it directly to the mistress of the house, apprising her of your presence. If you are informed that the mistress of the house is otherwise engaged, accept this news placidly and do not attempt an interrogation. Leave your calling card and two of your husband's, one of his being for the hostess and the other for her husband.

If you are calling to accept or decline to an invitation, and you find that the mistress of the house is unavailable, it is bad form to write "regrets" or "accepts" upon your card. A note of reply must always be written in acknowledgement of an invitation.

DUTIES OF THE HOSTESS

It is not necessary for the hostess to advance to receive her visitors, unless it is someone to whom she is especially desirous of showing respect. She will rise, move forward a single step, and remain standing until they are seated.

If several ladies arrive at the same time, pay due respect to age and rank, and seat them in the most honorable places. In wintertime, these places are beside the fire.

If an acquaintance calls after a long delay, it is a duty to welcome her cordially, to hasten to accept any explanation she may offer, and not to allude to it again.

Never introduce morning visitors who happen to encounter each other in your parlor, unless they are persons from whom you have already obtained permission to make known to each other. When it is appropriate to introduce your guests to each other, always introduce the younger one to the elder.

If you wish your conversation to be thoroughly agreeable, lead a mother to talk of her children, a young lady of her last ball, or an artist of his works of exhibition.

A well-bred lady who is receiving several visitors at a time pays equal attention to all, and attempts, as much as possible, to generalize the conversation, turning to all in succession. She guides conversation as the four-in-hand driver manages his team, keeping all in order and up to their work.

It is a good plan to have books and pictures on the center table, and scattered about your parlors. You must, of course, converse with each caller, but many will remain in the room for a long time, and these trifles are excellent diversions, and serve as subjects for conversation.

It is a pleasant fashion to serve tea from the hours of 4:00 P.M. to 5:00 P.M. This cordial custom puts people at their ease and makes one's receiving day popular.

You should always appear delighted to receive visitors.

FAUX PAS

TO BE AVOIDED BY THE SOCIAL CALL HOSTESS

 When friends come to call on you, don't look at your watch, lest they think you desire them to leave.

 Do not, if you are married, permit a gentleman to call upon you without the knowledge and full permission of your husband.

 Any absorbing occupation, like music or drawing, should be abandoned. When a particular friend is present for only a short time, it is inconsistent with etiquette to keep your eyes fixed on a crochet or knitting-book, apparently engaged in counting stitches, or unfolding the intricacies of a pattern.

 It is unreasonable to fancy that one's acquaintance is not desired because a call has not been returned promptly. Illness in the family, absence from town, or other occupations, may prevent the best-intentioned persons from making calls.

 Charity and etiquette commands a lady never to insult another in her own home, no matter how much she may dislike the visitor; and it is the very acme of ill-breeding to do otherwise.

 A hostess should never speak disrespectfully of those who have previously called.

DUTIES OF THE CALLER

Salute your hostess immediately upon entering the drawing room, bearing in mind that the salutation is the touchstone of good breeding. There have been men from time immemorial who have owed their ruin to a bad bow.

The hostess will indicate where you are to sit. Should she fail to do so, do not trouble her over the matter, but quietly seat yourself.

Ladies and gentlemen alike will always rise to their feet when an older person, or one of higher social standing, enters the room.

Restrain yourself from staying longer than ten to twenty minutes, which is the usual length for a call. In any event, a call should never exceed half an hour, even if the conversation should have become animated. It is better to let your friends regret, rather than desire, your withdrawal.

Should you be introduced to another visitor in the parlor of your hostess, converse with ease and freedom, as if you were acquainted. To be silent and stiff on such an occasion would show much ignorance and ill-breeding. That you are both friends of the hostess is sufficient guarantee of the other visitor's respectability.

In order to meet the general needs of conversation in society, it is necessary that a lady should be acquainted with the current news and historical events of at least the last few years.

Make your conversation bright and witty. If you cannot be animated, sympathetic, and cheerful do not go into society. Dull and stupid people are but so many clogs to the machinery of social life.

If you have occasion to look at your watch during a call, ask permission to do so, and apologize for it on the plea of other appointments.

When speaking to others of your husband or wife, do not refer to them by first name, but always as "Mr. _____" or "Mrs. _____."

You must endeavor to seem interested in the conversation of others.

FAUX PAS

TO BE AVOIDED BY SOCIAL CALLERS

Never intrude upon your friends in the early morning hours, as they usually have duties to attend to at that time.

Do not take along a dog to accompany you.

Never call upon a wet day. That said, umbrellas should inevitably be left in the hall.

Never sit gazing curiously around the room during a visit, as if taking a mental inventory of the furniture.

Do not finger the ornaments.

Do not discuss literature in a visit of condolence, nor lecture on political economy in a visit of congratulations.

TO BE ESPECIALLY AVOIDED BY LADY CALLERS

A lady should never call upon a gentleman, unless officially, as in the case of a parishioner consulting her clergyman. Otherwise, it is not only ill-bred, but positively improper to do so.

Do not use a loud voice; this is both disagreeable and vulgar. There is a certain distinct but subdued tone of voice that is peculiar to only well-bred persons. If you must err, do so by too low, rather than too loud, a tone.

Remember that all slang is vulgar. There are many ladies who pride themselves on the saucy chic with which they adopt certain slang words, and other cant phrases of the day. Such habits cannot be too severely reprehended. They lower the tone of society and the standard of thought. It is a great mistake to suppose that slang is in any way a substitute for wit.

FAUX PAS

TO BE ESPECIALLY AVOIDED BY GENTLEMEN CALLERS

 If you are going into the presence of ladies, beware of onions, spirits, and tobacco.

Do not use a classical quotation in the presence of ladies without apologizing for, or translating it.

Do not leave your hat and riding whip in the hall, but take both into the drawing room. To do otherwise would be to make yourself too much at home.

 A gentleman never sits in the house with his hat on in the presence of ladies for a single moment. Indeed, so strong is the habit that a gentleman will quite unconsciously remove his hat on entering a parlor, or drawing room, even if there is no one present but himself. Those who fail to observe this convention are to be suspected of having spent most of their time in barrooms and similar places.

Do not seat yourself beside the hostess, unless she invites you to do so.

Do not place your arm on the back of a chair occupied by a lady.

Concluding the Call

For the Hostess

At the conclusion of the visit, the hostess eases her caller's departure by making a tacit invitation to retire. She may allow the conversation to lapse without attempting to revive it, or arise from her seat on one pretext or another. This provides an opportunity for the guest to gracefully make her salutation and withdraw.

As each guest departs, the hostess rises, if she has not already done so, and remains standing until the guest has quite left the room. She should ring the bell in good time for the servant to let the guest out of the house.

For the Callers

If other visitors are announced, and you have already remained as long as courtesy requires, wait till they are seated, and then rise from your chair, take leave of your hostess, and bow politely to the newly arrived guests.

Never resume your seat after you begin to depart, no matter how strongly you may be urged. Nothing exhibits greater gaucherie than to sit down and start all over again after having said good-bye.

THE EXTENDED VISIT

A weekend house party in a large country house, where there is riding, motoring, boating, tennis, golf, skating, or other out of door amusements, is a jolly affair.

However, even a humble cottage may recommend itself as a venue for an agreeable visit of a few days' time. For in the end, it is not lavish entertainments, but the many small courtesies that one friend gladly offers another, which strike deepest to the grateful and appreciating heart.

Issuing and Accepting Extended Visit Invitations

For the Host and Hostess

When guests are invited to stay in the house, it is now the custom to ask them for a definite time— a weekend, a week, or a fortnight.

When inviting friends to visits of a week or more, try to fix the time for the visit to begin the day after the ironing is done. The servant feels a weight off her mind, has time to prepare the meals better, and is a much more willing attendant upon the guests.

If travelling by train, the guest should be told which train to take, and then be met at the station.

For the Guests

Never make a visit on general invitation. If persons really desire you to make a visit, they will make the invitation special and set the time. An effusive cordiality in extending invitations is not always to be taken at its face value.

A husband may be supposed to be included in an invitation to the wife, but not children and servants, unless they are specially mentioned.

Answer all invitations to visit immediately, whether you accept or not.

To postpone a visit or break the engagement for trivial reasons is the height of rudeness. In this day of many interests and duties for women, a hostess pays you a compliment to invite you at all.

DUTIES OF THE HOST AND HOSTESS

Those who receive "staying visitors," as they are called, should have a comfortable room awaiting the guest, with bed linen that is fresh and well aired, and a table furnished with writing materials and reading matter.

Meet your guest at the depot with your carriage, if possible. Attend to securing the baggage and having it sent to your residence without troubling him about it.

The surest way of making a guest happy is to find out what gives him pleasure, not to impose upon him what is pleasurable to you.

If you have more than one guest in your house, those of the humblest condition are to receive as much attention as the rest, in order that you shall not painfully make them feel inferior.

During the interval of the visit, the hostess should decline any invitations that exclude the guest.

Always ask to be excused while reading letters or papers in the presence of others.

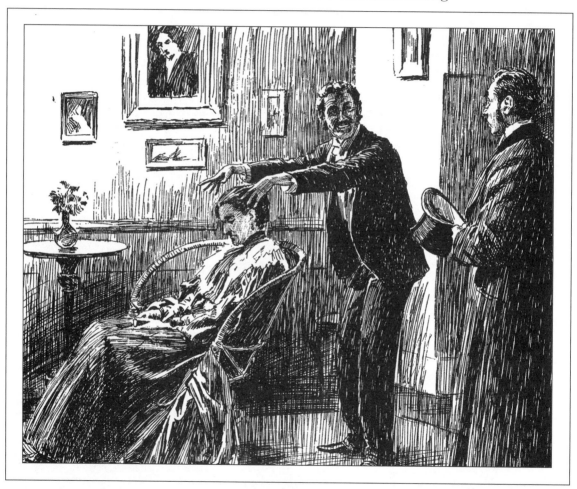

FAUX PAS

TO BE AVOIDED BY THE HOST AND HOSTESS OF OVERNIGHT VISITORS

Never send your guest, who is accustomed to a warm room, off into a cold, damp, spare bed to sleep.

Do not let it appear that you are making unusual efforts to be entertaining, but enter into the enjoyment yourself with a zest that shall put your visitor at his ease. If you let a visitor perceive that the whole tenor of your daily concerns is altered on his account, it is certain that he will feel a degree of depression.

It is always improper to engage in fondlings or familiarities when others are present. Spouses who entertain staying guests in their home must scrupulously avoid expressions of conjugal affection before company.

DUTIES OF THE GUESTS

A guest should appear promptly at meals, disarrange none of the habits of the family, nor ask extra attention from the servants. She should be blind and deaf to anything disagreeable that happens, and should not gossip afterwards about the private affairs of the hostess.

Do not presume upon the hostess before luncheon. Where people entertain a great deal the hostess is usually engaged during the morning, as she needs time to rest and attend to her duties.

When staying with friends on a Sunday, it is correct to appear at breakfast in the same dress that you intend to wear to church. To put on another dress for so short a time would be foolish.

Always treat with care and consideration the servants, the children, the horses, and the property generally, of those whom you are visiting.

Whatever entertainment may be offered you by your host or hostess should be entered into with spirit and zest. The company or amusement may not be just to your liking, but it is only a proper return for your friend's hospitality to appear to be entertained, even when you are not.

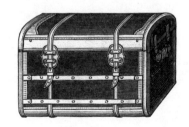

FAUX PAS

TO BE AVOIDED BY OVERNIGHT VISITORS

☞ Do not let your visit exceed a week; three or four days are usually enough.

☞ It shows the worst of breeding for a visitor to seclude herself from the family and seek her own amusements and occupations regardless of their desire to join in them or entertain her. Such a guest had better go to a hotel, where she can live as independently as she chooses.

☞ Never invite a friend who may call upon you to remain to a meal. This is an unwarrantable liberty in the house of another.

☞ Never make unfavorable comments about your friends' friends, nor, indeed, criticize unfavorably anything which you know them to favor or admire.

☞ Never betray any family secret that you may come to know through visiting in a house.

FAUX PAS

TO BE ESPECIALLY AVOIDED BY LADY VISITORS

While she is a visiting guest, a lady should not accept invitations that do not include the hostess.

It is not well for a lady guest to receive too many visits from gentlemen, or to accept any invitations from them without consulting her hostess as to her views upon it.

All ornaments in the morning are likely to be viewed as in very bad taste.

Should you take a child with you on a visit, be exceedingly watchful that she does not spoil the furniture with greasy fingers or break costly bric-a-brac, or do any of the thousand-and-one mischievous tricks that sometimes tend to render a child the most unwelcome visitor in the world.

DISINHERITED
SELFISH
BAD TEMPERED
AND
UNREASONABLE

CONCLUDING THE VISIT

For the Host and Hostess

When the time for departure has been finally fixed upon, no obstacles should be placed in the way of leave-taking.

Help your guest in every possible way to depart, packing her lunch, accompanying her to the station, and so on. Do not omit, however, to give a general invitation to renew the visit at some future period.

For the Guests

An act of courtesy that usually suggests itself to a thoughtful guest is the bestowal of some gift as a memento of the visit. This may be some piece of her own handiwork, if a lady guest, or flowers, a piece of jewelry, or anything small, pretty, and artistic.

Always write to your hostess immediately upon your return home, informing her of your safe arrival, thanking her for her hospitality, and expressing great enjoyment in your visit. Ask to be remembered to all the family, recalling each by name.

Do not fail to return the kindness of those who have extended you their hospitality. City people are delighted to visit the country, but far too seldom does it occur to them to invite their country friends to visit them in the city. Unwillingness to return hospitality is just plain selfishness, and people who are guilty of it are properly rebuked by not being invited for a return visit.

LADIES' AFTERNOON ENTERTAINMENTS

THE TEA PARTY

iven generally exclusively for ladies, the afternoon tea party constitutes a delightful entertainment for hostess and guests alike. Gone are the anxieties, the formality, and the etiquette of the dinner table. Light and not unduly complicated, the refreshments do not tax the delicate female digestive system. All ostentatious display is avoided. And, as the interval is brief, ladies are little apt to succumb to the subsequent malaise so often induced by the rigors of evening parties. In short, as no less a connoisseur of elegance and decorum than Henry James has written, "there are few hours in life more agreeable than the hour dedicated to the ceremony known as afternoon tea."

Issuing and Accepting Tea Party Invitations

For the Hostess

The hours of the afternoon tea party are from 4:00 P.M. to 6:00 P.M. This is of strictest importance, as an affair which continues into the evening hours will of necessity partake of the nature of a more formal entertainment. The invitation is informal and may be delivered a fortnight, a week, or a day or two in advance of the event. You may print it on large-sized visiting cards from engraved plates, as follows:

> *Mrs. Jane Smith*
> *Thursday, January 16, 1890*
> *298 Main Street*
> *from 4 until 6 o'clock*

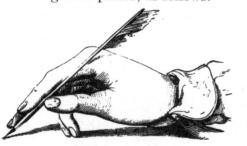

In the alternative, your invitation may take the form of a friendly note, something in this manner: *"Dear Miss Jones, We have some friends coming to drink tea with us tomorrow; will you give us the pleasure of your company also? We hope you will not disappoint us."*

Six is about the right number for a small tea party.

An invitation that refers specifically to tea need not include the hours, which will already be known to any lady of good breeding.

Always use the phrase "drink tea" rather than "take tea," as the latter is considered a vulgarism.

For the Guests

It is well to ascertain in advance of the party whether it is the local custom for each lady to bring her own cup. If such is the case, the cup will be carried to the tea, carefully wrapped, in a special box.

It is considered very rude to refuse an invitation to tea. However, if you must do so, you are obliged to call on your hostess within two days of the tea, which you were unable to attend. Tender your sincere regrets; inquire, as you would in the course of any call, after all the inmates of the house; introduce some small topic of agreeable conversation; and take your leave within ten or twenty minutes' time. In this way, the hostess is given to understand that you intended no offense, and cordial relations are maintained.

DRESSING FOR THE TEA

For the Hostess

Proper dress for the hostess will vary with the social position and means of the wearer. In general, it is well that her dress be of silk or other goods suitable to the season, but of plain colors. Lace is permissible, as is a certain amount of jewelry.

For the Guests

Guests wear spruce morning dress, with as much or as little display of train and bonnet as may suit their views. In some circles, the ladies customarily dress themselves in luxurious lace-trimmed tea gowns known as "teagies," with or without a train. Of special interest to many ladies is the happy fact that a tea gown may be worn *sans* corset. Gloves are also an essential part of the attire.

PREPARING FOR THE TEA

At a small afternoon tea, tea and perhaps coffee may be served in the dining room with guests seated around the tea table. For larger affairs, tea is handed round in the drawing room and the guests help themselves to refreshments from a buffet. It is not unusual for guests to stand, most especially when there are many of them and few chairs.

Only simple refreshments should be served. The bill of fare may consist exclusively of thin slices of bread and butter and cake.

Biscuits, sandwiches, fresh fruit, chocolate, consommé, and ice cream may also be offered. Punch and lemonade may be added if desired; and also salted almonds, candies, and other dainty trifles. Although the refreshments are simple, care must be taken that they are of the very best quality. No wine of any kind should be offered.

Bread-and-butter is carefully rolled so that none of the butter appears upon the exterior of the bread. In this manner it will be found possible to partake of it without removing the gloves, which is frequently a task of some difficulty. In fact, it is of so much difficulty that, rather than undertake it, the visitor often takes her tea without eating any, a practice which the doctors consider to be very injurious to the digestive organs.

Lemon, if offered with tea, is to be cut into slices, never into "wedges."

In setting a tea table, small-sized plates are set around, with a knife, napkin, and butter-plate laid by each in a regular manner; while the articles of food are to be set, also, in regular order. On the side table are placed teacups and saucers, sugar bowl, slop-bowl, cream cup, and a pot of hot water with which guests may weaken their tea, if so desired.

Afternoon tea is sometimes known as low tea, as it is served at the low point of the afternoon, about 4:00 P.M. What is known as a high tea is a meal taking the place of dinner, served at about 5:00 P.M., at which hot meats, cakes, warm breads, preserves, and other sweets are served. High teas are more popular in the country than in town.

BREWING TEA

Of all cups that cheer, there is nothing like the smoking-hot cup of tea, made with boiling water, in a thoroughly scalded teapot. The best teapot is that which retains heat the longest, and this is a bright metal one, as it radiates the least heat, but the metal must be kept bright and polished.

Having chosen your teapot wisely, put into it the required amount of tea. One teaspoon of tea leaves is the usual allowance for each person. Then pour over it boiling water, of which one cup for each person should suffice. Cover the teapot so that no steam may escape, and allow the tea to stand and infuse for seven minutes, when it should be poured at once into cups. If allowed to infuse longer than this time, which is sufficient to draw out the strength of the leaf, the tannin is developed, which gives an acrid, bitter taste, and being a powerful astringent, is destructive to the coating of the stomach.

To insure the tea remains hot while serving, in a different teapot from that in which the tea is made, cover the teapot with a quilted cloth or "bonnet" made specifically for that purpose. This is a sure preventive against that most insipid of all drinks—a warmish cup of tea.

As the Tea Begins

For the Hostess

Make sure you are dressed at least a half-hour before your guests are to arrive. To come in, flushed from a hurried toilette, to meet your first callers, is unbecoming as well as rude.

As each visitor is announced, rise, advance part of the way to meet her, give her your hand, and welcome her cordially. Any formality is out of place on an informal occasion.

If the number of guests is small, you should walk about the room, talking with your visitors. If large, it is best to remain near the door, and have the aid of other ladies, who should entertain the guests, ask them to take refreshments, and make introductions when necessary.

Should you see two unacquainted ladies in proximity with one another, and with no one else near them with whom they can converse, you will introduce them to each other, provided that you think such a course would be agreeable to both of them. Two or three moments spent in starting them upon some subject congenial to both will not be wasted.

For the Guests

Ladies treat ladies as gentlemen do each other. The visitor salutes her hostess first and last.

Unless you are among the first to arrive, you will find a cheerful and broken-up assemblage—people conversing in twos, or at most in threes. Join the discourse in a chatty, agreeable way.

Do not remove your hat. Inconvenient as the custom may be, ladies retain their hats or bonnets throughout the tea, and likewise their gloves.

Pouring and Drinking Tea

For the Hostess

Unless the party is quite large, the hostess makes and dispenses the tea, and no servant is employed to hand round the cups. Any young girls who are friends of the hostess will volunteer to assist her. If there should chance to be any gentlemen present, they would naturally undertake the task of giving each lady her cup of tea, handing her the bread-and-butter or cake, and taking her cup from her when it is empty.

The hostess inquires of each guest how many spoons of sugar she wishes, making this addition prior to pouring the tea. Lemon slices, if such are desired, are placed in the cup subsequent to the tea having been poured.

Both cream and milk may also be offered; in their absence, the white of an egg beaten to a froth, with a small bit of butter well mixed with it, may be used.

For the Guests

Here is the proper way to hold your teacup. First, slip your index finger through the handle, up to almost the first knuckle. Then balance and secure the cup by placing your thumb on the top of the handle and allowing the bottom of the handle to rest on your middle finger.

After stirring, place your spoon quietly on the saucer, behind the cup, on the right hand side under the handle.

If you are standing or seated away from the table, lift the teacup with the saucer when drinking. If you are seated at a table, you may leave the saucer on the table.

When you wish to be served more tea, place your spoon in your saucer. If you have had a sufficient amount, let the spoon remain in the cup.

TO BE AVOIDED BY TEA PARTY GUESTS

 Request no more than one or two spoonfuls of sugar with your tea. Although you may customarily take more, it is ill-bred and appears greedy to do so at the table of another.

 Do not essay the addition of milk or cream to tea that already contains lemon; the result will be a curdled mess which is unpleasant to behold and impossible to drink.

 Tea and coffee should never be poured into a saucer.

 It is not proper to drink with a spoon in the cup, nor should one, by the way, ever quite drain a cup or glass.

 When you drink, don't elevate your cup as if you were going to stand it inverted on your nose. Bring the cup perpendicularly to the lips, and then lift it easily to a slight angle.

 Do not extend your ring and small fingers upward; this is an affectation, which bespeaks arrogance, not refinement.

 Do not allow the spoon to clink noisily against the sides of the cup as you stir your tea.

 Do not sip your tea from the spoon.

 Do not slurp your tea, nor use it to wash down a large bite of food.

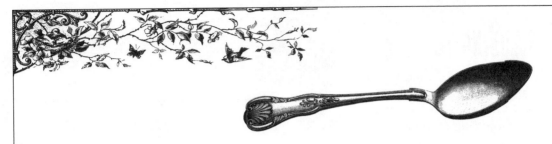

☞ Do not peek over the cup at others while you are sipping. Lower your eyes and look into your cup.

☞ Do not overindulge. Black tea, when taken to excess, so acts on the nervous system as to produce sleeplessness and insomnia, and finally makes a complete wreck of its victim.

☞ Never help yourself to butter or any other food with your own knife and fork.

☞ Do not bite a cream cake, but eat it with knife and fork. As for the knife, ladies have frequently an affected way of holding it halfway down its length as if it were too big for their little hands, but this is as awkward a way as it is weak. The knife should be grasped freely by the handle only, the forefinger being the only one to touch the blade, and that only along the back of the blade at its root and no further down.

CONCLUDING THE TEA

No guest should remain at a tea party longer than thirty to forty-five minutes. It is a mark of good breeding to very quietly take leave of the hostess and vanish without disturbance.

It is ever the done thing to pay a brief call, no more than ten to twenty minutes in duration, upon the hostess within the week. Express your enjoyment of the occasion, compliment any aspect that you found especially delightful, and be gone.

THE LUNCHEON

adies' luncheons are such sociable affairs that they are very popular with many who dread the ceremony of a dinner, and yet who desire to entertain their friends. Any meal between the regular ones is called a luncheon. However, the ladies' luncheon is usually given about one o'clock, and, while similar to a dinner party, is not so heavy. The hostess may make this meal as simple or as elegant she chooses.

ISSUING AND ACCEPTING LUNCHEON INVITATIONS

The invitations may be given by card, or even verbally. They should be delivered four days to two weeks in advance of the event.

A lady who has been invited to a luncheon should accept immediately. She is obligated to send word at once if, after accepting an invitation, any sudden occurrence prevents her from attending.

DRESSING FOR THE LUNCHEON

For the Hostess

Ladies' luncheons are the least formal of all social occasions, a fact which should be reflected in your attire. For all but the fanciest of affairs, a pretty dress of the sort you wear to receive your morning calls will serve nicely. Naturally, you will wish to look well, but take pains that your attire does not eclipse that of your guests. In dress, as in all other things, let consideration for others be your guide.

For the Guests

Wear an attractive street gown with wrap, bonnet, and gloves, just as you would when paying a call. No matter how becoming, your tea gowns have no place at a ladies' luncheon; save them for the proper occasion.

SETTING THE TABLE

As the guests arrive, your well-polished table should be only partially covered with a handsome centerpiece, doilies under plates and glasses, and dishes containing fruit. At a very informal party, the sweets may also be placed on the table in advance. All platters containing food, however, should be placed on a side table to be served after the guests have been seated.

For a very large lunch party, several little tables may be used in place of one long one. If such is the case, take care that the servants have ample room to pass between the tables.

At formal lunches it is a genteel custom to provide a bouquet for each lady, they being grouped as an ornament in the center of the table, and distributed after the meal. Occasionally, also, some pretty trifle is given to each guest as a memento of the occasion, but there is no obligation for this to be done.

COMMENCING THE LUNCHEON

For the Hostess

As your guests enter the drawing room, greet them warmly and ask them to take a seat. If it happens that any lady should be tardy, do not delay having the luncheon served on her account, as this would unfairly inconvenience those who arrived at the appointed hour. Invite your guests into the dining room with a few graceful words, then lead the way. Your place is at the head of the table.

For the Guests

Remain seated in the drawing room until invited to enter the dining room. As there are no gentlemen present to serve as escorts, each lady walks in separately rather than arm-in-arm with another. Guests may sit wherever they please.

SERVING THE LUNCHEON

At an informal luncheon party, the hostess helps serve the cold meats or other main course. The guests help themselves to the other dishes, and also help each other when it is polite to do so. Of course, at a larger party servants serve the meal.

From three to five courses are sufficient. The first course should consist of fruit or raw oysters. Boneless and jellied meats are very popular as a main course. Many persons never serve vegetables at an informal lunch, and the utmost freedom of choice in the selection of dishes is allowable. Water and lemonade or punch should be offered by way of liquid refreshments. It is customary to conclude this light afternoon meal with an elegant luncheon cake of the sort containing raisins, almonds, caraway seeds, currants, nutmegs, and peel.

When there are several courses, the plates should be changed at each course.

Ladies' Afternoon Entertainments

FAUX PAS

TO BE AVOIDED BY THE LUNCHEON HOSTESS

 It is not considered proper for ladies to remove their jackets, hats, or bonnets at luncheon. Be wary, therefore, of providing dishes that require much manipulation on the part of the diner. Do not serve soup, fish, or other comestibles that might easily soil the gloves of your guests.

Tea and coffee are never served at or after luncheon.

TO BE AVOIDED BY THE LUNCHEON GUESTS

 Both etiquette and good feeling forbid gossip or scandal at a ladies' lunch party, and nothing is more ill-bred than to afterward make ill-natured criticisms upon the hostess or the entertainment she has provided.

Concluding the Luncheon

For the Hostess

Following the luncheon, invite your guests into the drawing room. You may, if you wish, invite musically inclined guests to sing or play for a few minutes.

For the Guests

Take your leave no more than twenty minutes after settling in the dining room. Do not linger upon saying farewell. It is not necessary to be rudely abrupt, but in saying good-bye, the sooner it is over the better for all concerned. Suspense is painful to the parties, and tiresome to spectators.

THE DINNER PARTY

 inner has been pronounced to be, in civilized life, the most important hour of the twenty-four. It has also been said that the worst torture that survives the inquisition is a bad formal dinner. To give a large, successful dinner party, then, with every detail in good form, is perhaps the severest test of a lady's talents and social experience. Less numerous, yet also exacting, are the especial obligations of the guests. However, fear not, dear reader. When each and every member of the party, being fully apprised of his duties, strives to perform them with savoir-faire and grace, an elegant dinner may be justly counted among the most sublime of social occasions.

Issuing and Accepting Dinner Party Invitations

For the Host and Hostess

It is well to arrange a party in such a way that the number of ladies and gentlemen is equal.

To insure the likelihood of a most agreeable affair, select your guests from the same social circle and similar station of society.

Allow the size of your table to determine the number of guests. When the party is too small, conversation flags, and a general air of desolation pervades the table. When there are too many, everyone is inconvenienced.

When considering the compatibility of your guests, keep in mind that women of great genius will not necessarily be grand raconteurs, as such women are sometimes almost lacking in conversational powers. Likewise, brilliant writers are often very poor talkers—shy, dull, and silent, with no power of expression.

While nearly all other social invitations are given in the name of the hostess alone, the invitation to dinner is given in the joint name of the host and hostess.

Notes of invitation are written in the third person and in the simplest style, as follows: *"Mr. and Mrs. Smith request the pleasure of Mr. and Mrs. Carter's company at dinner, on Saturday, June 1, at 7:00 P.M."*

Invitations should be written upon small notepaper, which may have your initial or monogram stamped upon it.

Good taste forbids anything more. The envelope should match the sheet of paper.

The invitations should be sent from two days to two weeks in advance, depending on the grandeur of the occasion. Many ladies drive to the houses of the guests and have the footman deliver the invitations, to be certain that they reach their destination properly.

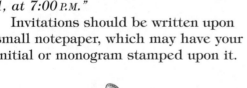

FAUX PAS

TO BE AVOIDED WHEN ISSUING DINNER PARTY INVITATIONS

☞ Do not invite too many members of one family.

☞ Do not ask the husband without the wife, or the wife without the husband.

☞ Do not allow the number at the table to total thirteen, for certain people have a superstition about this number; and though it is a very foolish and absurd one, it is courteous to respect it.

For the Guests

An invitation to dinner is the highest social compliment, and should be so received and treated.

You must reply immediately, and unequivocally accept or decline. Once accepted, nothing but an event of the last importance should cause you to fail to meet your engagement.

As with notes of invitation, notes of acceptance are written in the third person. The reply should be couched as follows: *"Mr. and Mrs. Carter have much pleasure in accepting Mr. and Mrs. Smith's kind invitation for Saturday evening, June 1."*

FAUX PAS

TO BE AVOIDED BY DINNER PARTY GUESTS

☞ Never refer to an invitation as an "invite." It is neither good breeding nor good English.

☞ Under no circumstances should you arrive late at a dinner party; this constitutes an utter outrage. If you do not reach the house until dinner is served, it is better to retire and send an apology than to interrupt the harmony of the courses by awkward excuses and cold acceptance.

☞ By the same token, you should not arrive excessively early. However, if by accident or thoughtlessness you arrive too soon, you may pretend that you called to inquire the exact hour at which they dine, having mislaid the invitation. You should then retire to walk for an appetite.

DRESSING FOR THE DINNER PARTY

For the Hostess

The hostess's dress should be rich in material, but subdued in tone, in order that she may not eclipse any of her guests. A young hostess should wear a dress of rich silk, black or dark in color, with collar and cuffs of fine lace, and plain jewelry, or, if the dinner is by gaslight, glittering stones. An elderly hostess may wear satin or velvet, or rich lace.

For the Lady Guests

The dress of a female guest at a dinner party is less showy than that for an opera or ball; still, it may be rich. Women may wear silks and velvets for winter. Light goods for summer, which may be worn over silk, are most appropriate.

FAUX PAS

TO BE AVOIDED BY LADIES WHEN DRESSING FOR A DINNER PARTY

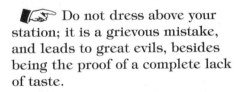

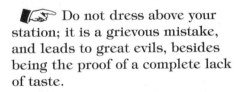 Do not dress above your station; it is a grievous mistake, and leads to great evils, besides being the proof of a complete lack of taste.

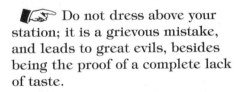 Do not expose the neck and arms at a dinner party. These should be covered, if not by the dress itself, then by lace or muslin overwaist.

 Do not fail to try the effect of your dress by gaslight and daylight both. Many a color that will look well in daylight may look extremely ugly in gaslight.

For the Host and Gentlemen Guests

When a gentleman is invited out for the evening, or when he hosts an evening entertainment himself, he is under no embarrassment as to what he shall wear. The unvarying uniform is black pants, waistcoat and jacket, with white tie, shirt, and gloves.

SETTING THE TABLE

The modern dinner table is made very attractive by an elaborate display of cut-flowers, which, taken with the requisite cut-glass and beautifully decorated china now in use, give an aesthetic aspect to what might be otherwise merely the gratification of a sensual appetite.

The most fashionable dinner service is of plain white with a small fillet of gold and the arms or crest and motto of the owner painted on the flat rim of the plates and dishes. The glasses should also be engraved with the same heraldic device.

The places should be evenly spaced and all arranged exactly alike. In the middle of each is a place plate, to be removed when the first course is served; alternatively, there is a place card that any clever high school girl can draw and decorate.

At the top of each place are arranged the spoons for the iced grapefruit, soup, dessert, and coffee. The napkin is placed at the right. Behind it is a small bread and butter plate. At the left is the dinner knife, and the forks placed in the order of their use— oysters, fish, roast, salad, game, dessert. If there is a second knife, it is meant to be used for separating bones from fish, or for cutting a green salad. Drinking glasses stand behind the forks in a row.

Under each chair should be placed a stool or hassock for ladies, or for such as may require it.

Ceremonious dinners are served in the modern fashion: that is, nothing is put on the table but the dessert, and all the other comestibles are served in courses by waiters. This mode has a decided advantage over the old method of putting the meats and vegetables on together, as it does away with the awkwardness and confusion of carving and serving, and keeps the table in a much neater condition.

The lady of the house should see that the appearance of the dessert is such that each dish, the fruit especially, should, with the help of flowers and leaves, be made into an elegant ornament. Fern leaves are well adapted for this purpose.

SEATING ARRANGEMENTS

Prior to the dinner party, the hostess will acquaint herself with the social standing of each guest. If necessary, she may consult a reference volume, such as *Who's Who*. She then pairs each gentleman guest with a lady guest of equivalent social status, whom the gentleman will escort to dinner and wait upon during the meal. The seating arrangements will be composed accordingly:

It is customary for the host and hostess to sit opposite one another, at the side of the table, in the center.

The two most distinguished gentlemen ought to be placed next to the mistress of the house, and the two most distinguished ladies next to the master of the house.

The right hand is especially the place of honor.

A space of two feet should be allowed to each person.

Husbands and wives should sit as far as possible from each other. Society is the enlargement, the absorption, and, for the time being, the breaking up of all private and exclusive engagements.

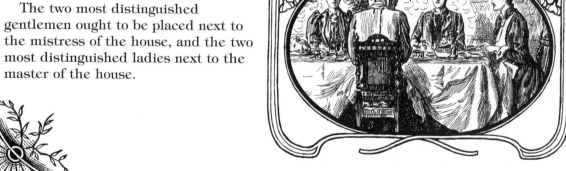

THE BEFORE-DINNER INTERVAL

The brief interval between the arrival of the guests and the commencement of dinner is passed in the parlor or drawing room.

For the Hostess

When guests are announced, the lady of the house advances a few steps to meet them, gives them her hand, and welcomes them cordially. If there are strangers in the company, it is best to introduce them to all present, that they may feel no embarrassment.

At some point before dinner is announced, the hostess will discreetly point out to each gentleman the lady he will escort to dinner. In the alternative, the hostess may address an envelope to each gentleman, enclose a small monogrammed card inscribed with the appropriate lady's name, and deposit the envelopes on a table in the gentlemen's dressing room.

For the Host

When dinner is announced, the host will take the principal lady guest on his right arm, invite the rest of the guests to follow by a few words or a bow, and lead the way to the table.

For the Guests

Guests should arrive fifteen or twenty minutes before the hour named in the invitation.

You should pay your respects to the hostess before you even greet any of your other friends who may be in the room. Once this courtesy is performed, you have the right to offer a civility, or the charm of your society, to any person present.

Do not entertain the notion that a gift to your host and hostess, even a small one, will be welcome at this time. Your gift might well be taken as an imputation on the lavishness of the hospitality offered.

Especially for the Gentlemen Guests

The most distinguished gentleman guest has the privilege of escorting the lady of the house to the dinner table.

If, when dinner is announced, a gentleman finds that the hostess has especially placed no lady under his care, he is to offer his arm to whichever lady he last conversed with.

Having arrived at the table, each gentleman respectfully bows to the lady whom he has conducted.

Especially for the Lady Guests

Ladies should politely take the arm of whichever gentleman, having been appointed to escort her to the dinner table, offers his.

Upon arriving at the table, the lady reciprocates the gentleman's bow.

And Finally . . .

The guests find their places by the names on the place cards and every one sits down in a gay flutter of talk and laughter.

The Delicate Art of Dinner-Table Conversation

Perfect good nature, and a certain degree of hilarity, befit every feast. The conversation should, therefore, be easy, playful, and mirthful.

The rules of politeness are never at variance with the principles of morality. Whatever is really impolite is really immoral. We have no right to offend people with our manners or conversation.

Conversation is general, but each guest is especially responsible for entertaining his partner.

If we believe a man to be unfit company for us, we must not invite him to our home, but if we meet him at a dinner party where he has been invited by others, we must treat him with civility.

TOPICS TO BE AVOIDED AT THE DINNER TABLE

☛ Do not quote Latin or Greek in the presence of those who may be presumed to be ignorant of either.

☛ Do not mention at the table anything that might not properly be placed upon it.

☛ Do not mention disease, or medicine, or anything connected with either. If one speaks of a voyage, he must omit the interesting fact of his having been seasick.

☛ Do not mention any topic, which could, directly or indirectly, excite disgust. Nor, must there be said anything to excite anger. This is, of course, the rule in all conversation; but it is especially dangerous to get angry over one's dinner. Therefore, do not discuss subjects such as politics and religion. People who are serious and thoughtful at the table are liable to become dyspeptics.

☛ Do not parade the fact that you have traveled in foreign countries.

☛ Do not boast that you are acquainted with distinguished or wealthy people.

☛ Do not mention that you have been to college, or that your family is distinguished for gentility and blue blood.

THE ETIQUETTE OF THE DINNER TABLE

Eat slowly; it will contribute to your good health as well as your good manners. Thorough mastication of your food is necessary to digestion.

Treat the waiters with courtesy, and say, "No, I thank you," or "If you please," in answer to their inquiries.

A few well-chosen words of praise for any dish that you happen to know is a matter of pride to your hostess will be well received. As a rule, however, the fewer remarks about your food, the better.

It is best to follow the old-established customs when taking dinner wines. You will be offered sherry or sauterne with soup or fish; hock and claret with roast meat; punch with turtle; champagne with whitebait; port with venison; port or burgundy with game; sparkling wines between the roast and the confectionery; Madeira with sweets; port with cheese; and for dessert, port, Tokay, Madeira, sherry, and claret.

Be moderate in the quantity you eat. You impair your health by overloading the stomach, and render yourself dull and stupid for hours after the meal.

TO BE AVOIDED AT THE DINNER TABLE

 Do not comment upon anything unpleasant you may find in your food, such as a hair in the bread or a fly in the coffee. Simply remove the offending item without remark. Though your own appetite be spoiled, it is well not to spoil that of others.

 Do not speak of "milk," no matter how watery and pale the fluid may be. Always remember to ask for "cream."

 Do not hesitate what to take when a dish is passed to you. Nothing displays a lack of breeding more than not to know your own mind in trifles.

 Do not refuse to take the last piece of bread or cake; it looks as though you imagined there might be no more.

 Do not carry anything like food with you from the table.

 Never leave the table before the end of the dinner, unless from urgent necessity.

The Dinner Party

FAUX PAS

TO BE ESPECIALLY AVOIDED BY LADIES AT THE DINNER TABLE

To be acquainted with every detail pertaining to dinner table etiquette is of the highest importance to every lady. Ease, savoir-faire, and good breeding are nowhere more indispensable than at the dinner table, and the absence of them is nowhere more apparent. How to eat soup and what to do with a cherry-stone are weighty considerations when taken as the index of social status; and it is not too much to say that a young woman who elected to take claret with her fish, or eat peas with her knife, would justly risk the punishment of being banished from good society.

Unless you are a total abstainer, it is extremely uncivil to decline taking wine if you are invited to do so. In accepting, you only have to pour a little fresh wine into your glass, look at the person who invited you, bow slightly, and take a sip from the glass.

Young ladies seldom drink more than three glasses of wine at dinner; but married ladies who are engaged in a profession, such as authors and teachers, and those accustomed to society and the habits of affluence, will habitually take five or even six, whether in their own homes or at the tables of their friends.

Do not wear gloves at the table.

FAUX PAS

TO BE ESPECIALLY AVOIDED BY GENTLEMEN AT THE DINNER TABLE

A man may pass muster by dressing well, and may sustain himself tolerably well in conversation; however, if he is not perfectly *au fait*, dinner will betray him.

Do not fail to give special attention to the cleanliness of your hands and fingernails. It is a great insult to every lady at the table for a man to sit down to dinner with his hands in a bad condition.

When a dish is brought to you, do not fail to see that the lady you have escorted to the table is provided for before you serve yourself.

Never offer to "assist" your neighbors to this or that dish. The word is inexpressibly vulgar—all the more vulgar for its affectation of elegance. "Shall I send you some mutton?" or "May I help you to grouse?" is better chosen and better bred.

Never pare an apple or pear for a lady unless she desire you to, and then be careful to use your fork to hold it; you may sometimes offer to divide a very large pear with or for a person.

DUTIES OF THE HOST AND HOSTESS

The Host

The dinner party host is expected to contribute much to the enjoyment of the guests.

His geniality lends warmth and brightness to the atmosphere, putting everyone at ease, while his refinement serves to set the proper tone. Courtesy demands that the host spread his good cheer among all members of the party, neither slighting those with whom he is not well acquainted, nor paying special attention to those with whom he is. If he is, by nature, a witty fellow, then by all means let his repartee augment—though never dominate—the general merriment.

As we have noted previously, the modern convention is that all carving be performed away from the table. If, however, the host still adheres to the custom of addressing the meats at the table, it is very essential that he should thoroughly understand how to carve.

The Hostess

The duties of the hostess at a dinner party are not onerous; however, they demand tact and good breeding, grace of bearing, and self-possession in no ordinary degree. She has no active duties to perform; however, she must neglect nothing, forget nothing, put all her guests at their ease, encourage the timid, draw out the silent, and pay every possible attention to the requirements of each and all around her. No accident must ruffle her temper. No disappointment must embarrass her. She must see her old china broken without a sigh, and her best glass shattered with a smile.

In short, she must have the genius of tact to perceive, and the genius of finesse to execute; ease and frankness of manner; a knowledge of the world that nothing can surprise; a calmness of temper than nothing can disturb; and a kindness of disposition that can never be exhausted.

The hostess ought never to appear to pride herself regarding what is on her table, nor apologize for any perceived deficiency thereof.

It is in poor taste to urge guests to load their plate against their inclination.

If a guest should upset a glass of grape juice or a cup of coffee, the hostess should be stone-blind to the accident. A trained waitress will come along casually and lay a napkin or doily over the stain.

If the hostess observes someone lingering over his plate, she shall appear to be eating, so that he may not make the mortifying discovery that he is the last to be eating.

If the hostess is a mother, she will be wise never to let her children make their appearance at dessert when she entertains friends at dinner. Children are out of place on these occasions. The guests only tolerate them through politeness; their presence interrupts the genial flow of after-dinner conversation; and with the exception of the hostess herself, and perhaps her husband, there is not a person at the table who does not wish them in the nursery.

Two hours is long enough to serve even the fanciest dinner; three hours and a half decidedly too long.

It is for the hostess to give the signal to leave the table.

The After-Dinner Interval

Contrary to the custom of low society, civilized gentlemen do not remain at the table after the ladies have retired, to indulge in wine, coarse conversation, and obscene jokes. The more enlightened practice is for ladies and gentlemen to retire together from the dining table.

Upon the signal of the hostess, all the guests rise, and, the gentlemen offering their arms to the ladies, wait upon them to the drawing room door.

It is expected that guests will linger for two or three hours after the dinner. In any event, no one may politely depart until at least one hour has passed. The after-dinner interval may be passed in conversation, or in various entertaining games. Guests must not now let lapse their obligation to converse in an amusing and entertaining fashion. Naturally, it is the height of rudeness to allow somnolence to overtake you during this time. Thus the thoughtful person has prudently avoided overindulgence in food or drink at the table.

TAKING LEAVE OF THE HOST AND HOSTESS

When it is time to depart, thank the hostess for a pleasant evening, but do not thank her for dinner. Shake the host's hand, if you are a gentleman, and bow yourself out. A lady does not shake hands in this circumstance; her gracious bow will suffice.

Within one week, pay a brief "dinner call" to express thanks to your host and hostess, and to briefly reminisce over the delights of the evening. Do not stay for less than ten minutes, or more than twenty.

AT HOME ENTERTAINMENTS

lmost every kind of social gathering may be properly termed an "At Home," with the exception of a dinner or a wedding breakfast. There are dancing At Homes, musical At Homes, and conversational At Homes, and any of these may take place in the afternoon or in the evening. No supper is served, but refreshments are provided in the dining room, to which the guests repair during the intervals of music, dancing, recitations, or the dramatic entertainments.

ISSUING AND ACCEPTING AT HOME INVITATIONS

For the Hostess

An evening At Home begins at about 9:00 P.M. and ends about midnight, or somewhat later. Notes of invitation should be written on small paper of the best quality, and enclosed in corresponding envelopes. Send your invitations from one to three weeks previous to the date, according to circumstances, so that the guests will have time to consider their engagements and prepare their dresses. All notes of invitation are issued in the name of the mistress of the house only, as follows:

Mrs. Green requests the honor of Mr. and Mrs. Smith's company at a small evening party on Monday, April 18.

In the alternative, you may purchase ready printed cards, with blanks for names or dates:

Mrs. Green at home,
Monday evening, April 18, instant

If there is any special feature that is to give character to the evening, it is best to mention this fact in the note of invitation. Thus the words "musical party," "to take part in dramatic readings," "to witness amateur theatricals," etc., should be inserted into the note. Let it be known, as well, if evening dress should be worn.

Should you propose a dancing party, pay due regard to the dancing qualifications of the proposed guests. One should be scrupulous and not wound the prejudices of a friend by sending her an invitation to such an affair when it is well known she is conscientiously opposed to dancing. A dancing party attended by more than fifty guests is properly termed a ball, and if you cannot afford to give one in good style, you had better not attempt it at all.

Should you wish to save yourself the bother and expense of issuing frequent invitations, you may merely send a card to all your friends, informing them that you are "at home" on some evening once a week. In this fashion, many a lady has gathered around her a most delightful society.

For a very simple evening party, to which ladies may wear summer walking dresses, the lady of the house gives verbal invitations, and does not omit to apprise her friends of this circumstance, or they might appear in unsuitable dresses.

For the Guests

Send your answer within a few days of receipt of the invitation. It is inconvenient for the hostess not to know how many guests she is likely to receive.

Your reply, like the invitation that occasioned it, should be written on plain paper of good quality. Eschew notepaper of even the most dainty and fastidious kind, although a lady may otherwise use it when writing to her friends and equals.

Never "avail" yourself of an invitation; the correct term is "accept." Phrase your response in the following fashion: *"Mr. Andrews has much pleasure in accepting Mrs. Green's polite invitation for Monday evening, April 18, instant."*

Should you decline the invitation, some reason must be given, the true cause—a prior engagement, a contemplated journey, sickness, domestic trouble, or whatever it may be—being stated clearly and concisely, so that the hostess shall have no possible occasion for offense.

DRESSING FOR THE AT HOME

For the Hostess

The hostess's dress should be rich, yet not ostentatious. It is never considered proper to outshine one's guests.

For the Lady Guests

For a small evening party, it is proper to dress as though paying an evening call. If the dress is low in the neck and with short sleeves, puffed illusion fabric should be used to cover the neck and arms. Wearing gloves is optional.

At a large evening party, ladies and gentlemen wear full evening dress, as to which no explicit directions can be given. The fashion-books declare what is to be worn, and the dressmaker is the interpreter of the fashion. However, it may be said that the richest velvets, the most expensive laces and elaborate headdress, the greatest display of gems, flowers, etc., shall belong to these occasions, likewise white kid gloves and satin boots.

It is best to aim at being as well dressed as the rest, yet not to outdo them or render one's self conspicuous.

Let it be remarked that if you go out to parties a great deal, you must vary your toilette as much as possible, lest idlers and malignant wits, who are always a majority in the world, should amuse themselves by making your dress the description of your person.

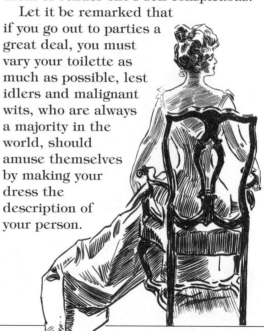

For the Host and Gentlemen Guests

Whether a gentleman be cast in the role of host or guest, sartorial correctness demands neither more nor less in the way of evening attire than black pants, waistcoat and jacket, white tie, shirt, and gloves. Nothing about a gentleman's appearance should excite any special observation, unless it be for neatness and propriety. It is in utmost poor taste for a gentleman to dress like a "dude" or "swell;" or to carry a little poodle dog (a man's glory is his strength and manliness—not in aping silly girls), or to wear anything conspicuous or that will make him offensive to others.

COMMENCING THE AT HOME

For the Host and Hostess

As the guests enter the room, it is not necessary for the lady of the house to advance each time toward the door, but merely to rise from her seat to receive their courtesies and congratulations.

In receiving guests, your first object should be to make them feel at home. Begging them to do so is not sufficient; you must display a genuine unaffected friendliness.

In making introductions, let tact and discretion be your guide. Some old-fashioned hosts yet persevere in introducing each newcomer to all the assembled guests. It is a custom that places the last unfortunate visitor in a singularly awkward position. All that she can do is to make a semicircular courtesy, like a concert singer before an audience, and bear the general gaze with as much composure as possible.

For the Guests

Guests are not obliged to arrive exactly at the appointed hour; it is even fashionable to arrive an hour later. Married ladies are accompanied by their husbands; unmarried ones, by their mother, or by an escort.

When entering a private party or ball, the visitor should invariably bow to the company.

Pay your respects to the hostess straightaway. She is generally to be found near the door. Should you, however, find yourself separated by a dense crowd of guests, you are at liberty to recognize those who are near you, and those whom you encounter as you make your way slowly through the throng.

DUTIES OF THE HOSTESS

The more really "at home" the hostess is, the better for her visitors, who come early or late, and stay as short or as long a time as they like.

In your own home, there is no impropriety in shaking hands with a new acquaintance. Do not, however, grasp a hand as though you desired to maim its possessor for life. On the other hand, a limp, flabby hand is about as pleasant to hold as a fish, and a lifted arm, drooped fingertips, and feeble wagging are an affected travesty. When both parties are gloved, it is not necessary to remove the glove, but if one only has a glove on, the other should remove her glove as well, unless the act of removing the glove would cause an awkward pause, in which case it would be sufficient to say simply, "Excuse my glove."

Refreshments are necessary, and not to have them would be the greatest impoliteness. Tea and coffee form the prominent features of these, and, in addition, wines and wine cups may be provided. You may offer also bread-and-butter, biscuits, cakes, sandwiches, fruit, or ices, just as you would at an afternoon tea.

Provide a full introduction to young ladies afflicted with shyness, apprising them of the special interests and talents of the person to whom they are being introduced. Suggesting a subject of conversation at once removes that awful pause which is so apt to ensue in such a case after the bows, and sets them at ease at once.

Never introduce a bad dancer to a good one. You have no right to punish one friend in order to oblige another.

You are the social queen in your home; accordingly, you are obliged not only to order, regulate, and govern your guests, but also to banish bores, disagreeables, and incompatibles from your society.

DUTIES OF THE HOST

Over all social festivities the lady of the house presides. She receives calls, gives invitations, welcomes the guests, and sits at the head of the table. The husband has only to devote himself to the ladies, and generally to the comfort of the guests.

In the case of a dancing party, the master of the house should see that all the ladies dance. He should take notice, particularly of those who seem to serve as drapery to the walls—or wallflowers, as the familiar expression is—and should see that they are

invited to dance. However, he must do this wholly unperceived, in order not to wound the self-esteem of the unfortunate ladies.

DUTIES OF THE GUESTS

In these assemblies, we should conduct ourselves with reserve and politeness towards all present, although they may be unknown to us. People who meet at a friend's house are ostensibly upon an equality, and pay a bad compliment to the host by appearing suspicious and formal.

If a man is tiresome, or becomes so by talking too much, the best way to escape is by a compliment. Thank him for the pleasure he has given, and do not deprive others of the benefit of listening to his instructive remarks.

If you possess any musical accomplishments, do not wait to be pressed and entreated by your hostess, but comply immediately when she pays you the compliment of inviting you to play or sing. Remember, however, that only the lady of the house has the right to ask you.

Be scrupulous to observe silence when any of the company are playing or singing. They are doing this for the amusement of the rest, and to talk at such a time is as ill-bred as if you were to turn your back upon a person who was talking to you and begin a conversation with someone else.

If you are the performer, bear in mind that in music, as in speech, brevity is the soul of wit. Two verses of a song, or four pages of a piece, are at all times enough to give pleasure.

When you cannot agree with the propositions advanced in general conversation, be silent.

FAUX PAS

TO BE AVOIDED BY GUESTS ATTENDING AT HOME ENTERTAINMENTS

 Do not remain too long in one spot. To be afraid to move from one drawing room to another is the sure sign of a neophyte in society.

 Do not query any person, especially a woman, on her age, or ask indirect questions with a view of discovering what her age really is. We must either advance in age, or we must die. Where, then, is the shame of surviving our youth?

 It is of gross impropriety and vulgarity to ridicule the aptitude of those who make musical offerings, engage in dancing, and the like. Those you condemn may not have had the same advantages as yourself in acquiring grace or dignity, yet may be infinitely superior in purity of heart and mental accomplishments.

 If you feel sad or ill, do not go into company. You have no right to depress others.

 Nothing is more ill-bred than a half-opened mouth, a vacant stare, a wandering eye, or a smile ready to break into a laugh at any moment. Absolute suppression of emotion, whether of anger, laughter, mortification or disappointment, is one of the most certain marks of good breeding.

 Never offer anyone the chair from which you have just risen, unless there be no other disengaged.

FAUX PAS

TO BE ESPECIALLY AVOIDED BY LADIES ATTENDING AT HOME ENTERTAINMENTS

Ladies of a certain age would do well to shun evening amusements of the livelier sort. Sad, indeed, is the condition of those in the decline of life still haunting balls and parties, and enduring all the discomforts of crowded watering places, long after all pleasure in such scenes must have passed away.

No very young lady should appear at an evening party without an escort.

A flippant "how-de-do" or a "happy-to-meet-you," said as mechanically as a talking doll would say it, does not recommend anyone to new acquaintance. Upon being introduced, you are not required to say anything—a smile and a bow are sufficient—and an air of deferential attention is more eloquent than many words.

A lady in company should never exhibit any anxiety to sing or play.

Do not, should you sit down to the piano to sing, twist yourself into so many contortions, and writhe body and face about into such actions and grimaces, as would almost incline one to believe that you are suffering great bodily torture. If amatory addresses are to be sung, let the expression be in the voice and the composition of the air, not in the looks and gestures of the lady singer.

FAUX PAS

TO BE ESPECIALLY AVOIDED BY GENTLEMEN ATTENDING AT HOME ENTERTAINMENTS

☞ Do not smoke shortly before entering the presence of ladies.

☞ Do not shake a lady's hand in a manner that would annoy her or hurt her fingers.

☞ Abstain from conversing with the members of the family at whose house the company are assembled, as they wish to be occupied with entertaining their other guests.

☞ Avoid talking to men, and devote yourself entirely to women, and especially to those who are not much attended to by others. All topics especially interesting to gentlemen, such as the farm and business matters generally, should be excluded in general society.

☞ If single, do not remain alone in a room with a lady who is likewise single, as this may leave you both open to embarrassment and possible speculation on the part of others.

CONCLUDING THE AT HOME

For the Host and Hostess

Take no offense at the early departure of any guest, as good breeding does not demand that they remain till the close of the evening. Rather, your visitors come and go as may be most convenient to them, and by these means are at liberty, during the height of the season when evening parties are numerous, to present themselves at two or three houses during a single evening.

You may expect, within the week, a brief visit of thanks from each of your guests.

For the Guests

In retiring from a crowded party it is unnecessary that you seek out the hostess for the purpose of bidding her a formal good night. By doing this you would, perhaps, remind others that it was getting late, and cause the party to break up. If you should meet the lady of the house on the way out, you should take your leave of her unobtrusively, and slip away without attracting the attention of her other guests.

Make to the master and mistress of the house, within the week, a visit of thanks of about ten to twenty minutes' duration. Converse therein of the pleasure of the evening and the good selection of the company.

Home Amusements

he spirit in which all home amusements should be conducted is to extract as much innocent fun as possible, avoiding everything rough and unseemly, or in which an exceptionally sensitive mind can find a cause of offense. With those who are simply boisterous in character, or have any element calculated to cause a feeling of annoyance or pain, ladies and gentlemen will have nothing to do.

Charades, Twenty Questions, Tableaux, and Shakespeare reading clubs constitute popular home amusements, and deservedly so, as they strengthen the lungs and memory, and improve the intellectual tastes. Private dramas amuse a large circle of friends, and some lady can almost always be found who will give the use of her house. Dominoes, checkers, chess, and all the various forms of card games generally form pleasant enough pursuits. In addition,  there exist such an abundance of common parlor games as to render impossible a complete accounting, though a modest list will be offered below.

DUTIES OF THE HOST AND HOSTESS

It is, by rights, the host or hostess who first proposes a game.

Neither host nor hostess may urge anyone who refuses to join in the amusement. The resistant guest may have conscientious scruples, and respect should be shown to their principles.

If it is determined to have charades at a party, the lady of the house should arrange dresses, plan of action, and subjects beforehand.

When weariness on any side commences, amusement is at an end. When there are symptoms of a game reaching that point, you must suggest that it be relinquished for another.

It falls to the host or hostess to provide new packs of cards.

DUTIES OF THE GUESTS

All who enter on games of this kind should be prepared to give as well as to receive amusement.

No one should refuse to play a game from mere caprice.

Play your best, and do not act indifferent to the game.

Do not talk on all manner of topics; it disturbs those who enjoy the game.

Never manifest anger at defeat, nor undue exultation at winning, nor lose your temper over a game.

Most games require that the participants select a good leader, who may be either a gentleman or a lady, as circumstances will admit. The principal qualification is knowledge of the game. If the person selected possesses, in addition, a commanding presence, ready wit,

brilliant imagination, and quick invention, so much the better. If not, he will probably get on very well without them.

Rudeness should be carefully avoided in every game, and especially towards the ladies.

To outshine others on every occasion is the surest road to unpopularity.

SOME COMMON PARLOR GAMES

Poor Pussy

One person, having been selected to enact the feline role, crawls on all fours amongst the other members of the party, who are seated on chairs. Eventually the selected person crouches at the feet of one particular person, fixes him with a pathetic gaze, and meows piteously. To this the seated person is obliged to respond with the phrase "Poor Pussy!" while betraying no hint of amusement. The game proceeds in this fashion until some respondent smiles or laughs, and must take the place of Poor Pussy.

The Ball of Wool

The participants are seated round a table, from which the cloth must be drawn. A little wool is rolled up into the form of a ball, and placed in the middle of the table. The company then commence to blow upon it, each one trying to drive it away from his own direction, and the object of all being to blow it off the table, so that the person by whose right side it falls may pay a forfeit. The longer the ball is kept on the table by the opposing puffs of the surrounding party, the more amusing the game becomes, as the zealous exertions of the players afford mirth to on-lookers as well as to themselves.

Composition

The host or hostess having first assembled adequate slips of paper and lead pencils as to provide for each member of the company, a leader is selected. Each member of the company then writes down a series of fifteen or so words, the majority of them nouns, provided by the leader. Everyone then has fifteen minutes to write a composition using every word mentioned. The leader

then reads each composition aloud, votes are taken as to which is best, and the lady or gentleman receiving the highest number of votes is entitled to a prize.

Blindman's Bluff

A member of the company is blindfolded and spun about five times. Meantime, each of the other players seeks a hiding spot within the room. At the conclusion of the fifth spin, the blindfolded player cries "Stop," upon which the other players are required to freeze in whatever position they may then be. The blindfolded player then attempts to locate each of the other players. For auditory assistance in ascertaining their whereabouts, he may periodically sing out "Blindman's—"; to

which the other parties are obligated to respond "Bluff."

The Courtiers

One of the company is selected to be king or queen, and occupies a chair in the center of the room, the rest being seated round the sides. The courtiers must imitate whatever movement may be made by the monarch; and it is the gist of the game that this should be done without any losing of decorous gravity which becomes the scene. The monarch may yawn, sneeze, blow his nose, or wipe his eye, and the courtiers must all do the same; however, if any one of them is so deficient in self-control or so presumptive as to grin or to laugh, he must pay the penalty of a forfeit.

FORFEITS

It will have been observed that many games lead up to the payment of penalties or forfeits, and that some appear to be designed for the express purpose of extracting as many as possible. This is really the case, for "crying the forfeits," as it is called, often forms the most amusing part of an evening's entertainment, and is, therefore, usually reserved until the last.

Each player who has to pay a forfeit deposits some small article—a handkerchief or a penknife, perhaps—with a person designated as collector. Two other persons, generally ladies, chosen from the rest of the company for their knowledge of a good number of suitable and amusing forfeits, then cry the forfeits. One lady is seated, and the various articles collected are placed in her lap. The other is blindfolded. (The object of the blindfolding is to prevent the recognition of any of the articles as belonging to particular members of the

company, and thus to assure impartiality in the allotment of the tasks.) As the seated lady raises each article, the blindfolded lady inquires whether it is a lady's or gentleman's article, and, having received an answer, declares the task which the owner must perform. Some popular forfeits follow:

Forfeits Suitable for a Gentleman

To go round the room blindfolded, and kiss all the ladies. The company, of course, are seated, but as soon as the gentleman is blindfolded they change positions, with as little commotion as possible.

He consequently finds, in his progress, that he as often attempts to kiss one of his own as one of the opposite sex; or a lady may reverse the position of her chair, so that the gentleman kisses the back of her head.

Say half a dozen flattering things to a lady, without using the letter "l." This may be done by such phrases as "you are pretty, "you are charming," etc., but such words as beautiful, graceful, and charitable are, of course, inadmissible.

To play the "learned pig." To do this, the gentleman must go on all fours, and then he is to answer questions put to him by the company, such as "show us the most agreeable person in the company," or "the most

charming," or "the greatest flirt," etc. After each question, the victim is to proceed to anyone whom he may select and signify his choice by a grunt. The learning as well as the docility of a pig has its limits, and the game must, therefore, not be prolonged too much.

Forfeits Suitable for a Lady

To say "yes" or "no" to three questions asked by the company. The lady must go out of the room, while the company agree as to each of the questions to be asked. To each of these questions the lady must give one or other of the plain monosyllables. Ladies of experience have intimated that the safe answer is always "no."

To sing a song, or play a piece of music. This is given either to elicit the musical capabilities of a lady who may be shy, or to make an agreeable interlude in the round of other forfeits. If the lady called upon can really do neither, another forfeit is allotted to her.

To repeat a proverb backwards. The lady may choose any proverb for the purpose.

Tableaux Vivants

A very delightful evening entertainment can be gotten up by having some interesting story read or poem recited. Meanwhile, its most picturesque portions are illustrated by a tableaux, the reader pausing while the curtain draws back revealing the dramatically grouped figures of the company, then continuing the story until there is another opportunity for an illustration. Of course, the management of the tableaux requires taste and skill, but with a little practice can be rendered very effective. Care should always be taken to avoid false lights, jarring colors, and unnatural positions.

Charades

There is no game that can afford so much amusement to a circle of friends of about twelve persons as that of acting charades. It affords a scope for the exercise of both wit and ingenuity. Yet, unless you have some real talent for acting and some readiness of speech, you should remember that you only put others out and expose your own inability by taking part. Of course, if your help is really needed, and you would disoblige by refusing, you must do your best, and by doing it as quietly and as coolly as possible, avoid being awkward or ridiculous.

FAUX PAS

TO BE ESPECIALLY AVOIDED WHEN PLAYING CARDS

 Married people should not play cards at the same table.

The fingers should not be too wet to deal the cards.

If a fourth hand is wanted at a rubber, or if the rest of the company sit down to a round game, do not decline to join. Under such circumstances, you would be deemed guilty of an impoliteness if you refused to play.

You have no right to sit down to the game unless you can bear a long run of bad luck with perfect composure. No well-bred person ever loses his temper at the card table.

Never let even politeness induce you to play for very high stakes.

Etiquette is the minor morality of life, but it never should be allowed to outweigh the higher code of right and wrong. To cheat is extremely ill-bred.

Index

fin